Contents

Introduction ....
Fact 1: The Sausage Dog Olympics Are a Real, Hilarious...
Fact 2: Sausage Dogs Were Designed for Digging...
Fact 3: The World's Longest Dog Tongue Belongs to a Dachshund 4
Fact 4: Dachshunds Have the Most Expressive Personalities 5
Fact 5: Dachshunds Have a Royal Pedigree 6
Fact 6: Dachshunds Are Natural Born "Spy Dogs" 7
Fact 7: Their Legs Might Be Short, But Their Dreams Are Big 8
Fact 8: Dachshunds Are Masters of the Guilt Trip 9
Fact 9: Their Dachshund "Bark" Sounds Like a Squeaky Toy 10
Fact 10: Dachshunds Were Popular Among Celebrities and Artists 11
Fact 11: Dachshunds Are Fearless—Even When They Shouldn't Be 12
Fact 12: Dachshunds Are Surprisingly Great Swimmers 13
Fact 13: Their Ears Have a Mind of Their Own 14
Fact 14: Dachshunds Have an Ancient Ancestry 15
Fact 15: Their Love for Sunbathing Makes Them Part-Time Cats 16
Fact 16: Dachshunds Are Definitely Not the "Lap Dog" 17
Fact 17: Dachshunds Have Their Own "Quirky" Personality Traits.. 18
Fact 18: Dachshunds Have an Incredible Sense of Smell 19
Fact 19: They Were Born to Dig—But Only When You're Watching 20
Fact 20: Dachshunds Are Surprisingly Great Athletes 21
Fact 21: Dachshunds Are Known for Their "Dachshund Dash" 22
Fact 22: Dachshunds Have a Strong "Bark" 23
Fact 23: Dachshunds Are the Best "Nap Buddies" 24
Fact 24: Dachshunds Can Be Very Vocal About Their Wants 25
Fact 25: Dachshunds Have a Unique Sense of Humor 26
Fact 26: Dachshunds Have a Rich History as Hunters 27
Fact 27: Dachshunds Have Big Dog Energy in a Small Dog's Body 28
Fact 28: Dachshunds Are Known for Their 'Dachshund Dance' 29
Fact 29: Dachshunds Are Surprisingly Good at Digging 30
Fact 30: Dachshunds Can Be Quite the "Drama Queens" 31
Fact 31: Dachshunds Are a Hit at Dog Parks 32
Fact 32: Dachshunds Have an Incredible Sense of Smell 33
Fact 33: Dachshunds Are the Masters of the "Guilty Face" 34
Fact 34: Dachshunds Have a Love Affair with Warmth 35
Fact 35: Dachshunds Are Natural Burrowers—Watch Out for Your Bed 36
Fact 36: Dachshunds Have a Serious Love for Car Rides 37
Fact 37: Dachshunds Can Be Quite the Foodies 38
Fact 38: Dachshunds Have a Sense of Humor 39
Fact 39: Dachshunds Love to Be the Center of Attention 40
Fact 40: Dachshunds Can Be Excellent Therapy Dogs 41
Fact 41: Dachshunds Love to Dig—It's in Their DNA 42
Fact 42: Dachshunds Are Surprisingly Agile for Their Size 43
Fact 43: Dachshunds Are Actually Very Protective of Their Family 44
Fact 44: Dachshunds Have a Tendency to Get "The Zoomies" 45

Fact 45: Dachshunds Have a Huge Appetite 46
Fact 46: Dachshunds Have the Best "Sad Eyes" in the Dog World 47
Fact 47: Dachshunds Are Surprisingly Vocal 48
Fact 48: Dachshunds Are "Lap Dogs" in Disguise 49
Fact 49: Dachshunds Have an Incredible Sense of Smell 50
Fact 50: Dachshunds Are Fearless (Even When They Shouldn't Be) 51
Fact 51: The Dachshund's Hidden Talent – Comedy Shows 52
Fact 52: The Art of Dachshund Manipulation 53
Fact 53: The Dachshund's Quest for Ultimate Comfort 54
Fact 54: The Dachshund's Obsession with Toys 55
Fact 55: Dachshunds and Their Love for Sunbathing 56
Fact 56: Dachshunds and Their Secret Career as Blanket Designers 57
Fact 57: Dachshunds and Their Fearless Approach to Life 58
Fact 58: Dachshunds and Their Inability to Handle Criticism 59
Fact 59: Dachshunds and Their Relationship with Food 60
Fact 60: Dachshunds and Their Unofficial Role as Alarm Systems 61
Fact 61: Dachshunds and Their Secret Talent for "Decorating" 62
Fact 62: Dachshunds and Their Love for Fashion 63
Fact 63: Dachshunds and Their "Selective" Hearing 64
Fact 64: Dachshunds and Their Rivalry with Cats 65
Fact 65: Dachshunds and Their Signature Waddle 66
Fact 66: Dachshunds and Their Obsession with Digging 67
Fact 67: Dachshunds and Their "Sausage Stretch" 68
Fact 68: Dachshunds and Their "Short-Legged" Speed Races 69
Fact 69: Dachshunds and Their Love-Hate Relationship with Baths 70
Fact 70: Dachshunds and Their Surprisingly Loud Voices 71
Fact 71: Dachshunds and Their "Houdini-Like" Escapes 72
Fact 72: Dachshunds and Their "Lap Dog" Aspirations 73
Fact 73: Dachshunds and Their "Guard Dog" Personalities 74
Fact 74: Dachshunds and Their Love for Blankets 75
Fact 75: Dachshunds and Their "Selective Hearing" 76
Fact 76: Dachshunds and Their Dramatic Side 77
Fact 77: Dachshunds and Their Food Obsession 78
Fact 78: Dachshunds and Their "Wiggle Walk" 79
Fact 79: Dachshunds and Their "Burrowing Olympics" 80
Fact 80: Dachshunds and Their Unique Sleeping Positions 81
Fact 81: Dachshunds and Their Love for Sunbathing 82
Fact 82: Dachshunds and Their "Prey Drive" Surprises 83
Fact 83: Dachshunds and Their Signature "Head Tilt" 84
Fact 84: Dachshunds and Their "Zoomies" 85
Fact 85: Dachshunds and Their Endless Curiosity 86
Fact 86: Dachshunds and Their "Doggy Drama" 87
Fact 87: Dachshunds and Their "Stretch Goals" 88
Fact 88: Dachshunds and Their Unique Vocal Range 89
Fact 89: Dachshunds and Their "Lap Dog Aspirations" 90
Fact 90: Dachshunds and Their "Fearless" Approach to Big Dogs 91

Fact 91: Dachshunds and Their Obsession with Food 92
Fact 92: Dachshunds and Their "Blanket Forts" 93
Fact 93: Dachshunds and Their Love-Hate Relationship with Water ... 94
Fact 94: Dachshunds and Their "Nap Time Rituals" 95
Fact 95: Dachshunds and Their "Sausage Dog Races" 96
Fact 96: Dachshunds and Their "Tail Wagging Adventures" 97
Fact 97: Dachshunds and Their "Protective Instincts" 98
Fact 98: Dachshunds and Their "Famous Fans" 99
Fact 99: Dachshunds and Their "Fashion Sense" 100
Fact 100: Dachshunds and Their "Infinite Charm" 101
Fact 101: Dachshunds and Their Legacy 102

Introduction

Welcome to 101 Sausage Dog Facts, your ultimate guide to the world of the beloved dachshund, affectionately known as the "sausage dog." Whether you're a seasoned dachshund owner, a curious animal lover, or simply someone who can't resist the adorable charm of these long-bodied, short-legged dogs, this book is for you. Here, we explore the delightful, quirky, and often hilarious traits of dachshunds, revealing everything you need to know about their history, personality, behavior, and the many ways they continue to capture our hearts.

Dachshunds are more than just a cute face with big ears and an endearing waddle. With their rich history, distinctive appearance, and sassy attitude, these little dogs have a way of making an impact on anyone who meets them. From their origins as courageous hunting dogs to their status as iconic companions and pop culture darlings, dachshunds have certainly earned their place as one of the most popular and unique dog breeds in the world.

In this book, you'll find 101 fascinating facts that will not only entertain you but also deepen your understanding and appreciation of these lovable little dogs. Prepare to be amazed as we dive into the unexpected, the funny, and the downright ridiculous behaviors that make dachshunds so special. You'll learn about their fearless nature, their hidden talents, and the hilarious antics that will leave you laughing and adoring them even more.

Each fact has been carefully crafted to give you a closer look at the dachshund's personality, history, and traits. We'll explore their enduring popularity, their role in our homes, and the delightful ways they've captured the hearts of millions around the globe. Whether you're here for the laughs, the love, or just to understand your dachshund a little better, we've got something for everyone. So grab a cozy spot, curl up with your furry friend, and enjoy this fun-filled journey into the world of the sausage dog. We hope this book not only brings a smile to your face but also helps you see your dachshund with fresh eyes, full of admiration and affection. Let's begin!

Fact 1: The Sausage Dog Olympics Are a Real, Hilarious Thing

Dachshund races, or "Wiener Dog Races," are an actual event that combines the cuteness of sausage dogs with the chaos of a kindergarten soccer game. From the Wiener Nationals in California to Germany's famous Dachshundrennen, these races are a beloved tradition for dachshund fans.

But let's not pretend these races are about athletic prowess. Watching a dachshund race is like herding drunk butterflies—adorable, chaotic, and completely unpredictable. While some dogs sprint with the focus of a greyhound, others forget they're in a race and stop halfway to sniff the grass, chase their tail, or say hello to spectators. And don't even get started on the costumes. Many dachshunds show up dressed as hot dogs (of course), superheroes, or even tiny chefs, adding an extra layer of hilarity to the event.

Yet beneath all the silliness, there's an undeniable charm to these races. They showcase the dachshund's boundless energy, quirky personality, and the absolute devotion of their owners, who cheer them on like proud parents. It's a reminder that in a world of sleek greyhounds and athletic retrievers, the humble sausage dog holds its own— with a dash of humor and a whole lot of heart.

Fact 2: Sausage Dogs Were Designed for Digging

If you've ever seen your dachshund burrow under a blanket, you're witnessing a behavior rooted in centuries of breeding. Dachshunds were specifically created to hunt badgers, and their long, flexible bodies, powerful legs, and paddle-shaped paws were perfectly suited for digging into burrows. In fact, their name comes from the German words dachs (badger) and hund (dog).

In the wild, a dachshund's job was simple yet daring: dive into badger dens, flush them out, and if necessary, engage in combat. Yes, dachshunds were bred to fight animals twice their size in pitch-black tunnels. This bravery, or perhaps sheer audacity, is still evident today. Ever notice how your sausage dog will try to "dig" into the couch, a pile of laundry, or even your lap? That's their inner badger hunter coming through.

Modern dachshunds might not hunt badgers anymore, but they've found new prey: your snacks, favorite blanket, and, occasionally, a hole in your backyard you swore wasn't there yesterday. Just remember—when a dachshund digs, it's not mischief. It's history.

Fact 3: The World's Longest Dog Tongue Belongs to a Dachshund

Believe it or not, dachshunds are record-breakers in more ways than one. Mochi, a dachshund from South Dakota, holds the Guinness World Record for the longest dog tongue, measuring an impressive 7.3 inches. That's longer than a can of soda!

Mochi's tongue is not just a quirky fact; it's a marvel of dachshund evolution. This tongue could lick peanut butter off a jar in one swipe or clean an entire plate with a single slurp. And let's be honest, it's impossible not to laugh when you see Mochi wagging his tail with his oversized tongue flopping around like it has a life of its own.

This record is a testament to the dachshund's unique charm. From their sausage-shaped bodies to their goofy grins (and, apparently, record-breaking tongues), these dogs never fail to stand out. Mochi's achievement reminds us that in the world of dogs, being a little extra is never a bad thing.

Fact 4: Dachshunds Have the Most Expressive Personalities in the Dog World

If dogs are man's best friend, dachshunds are man's most dramatic friend. These little divas wear their emotions on their sleeves—or rather, their wagging tails. When they're happy, they bounce around like furry pogo sticks. When they're sad, they sigh so loudly you'd think they've just been told there's no more bacon in the world.

And don't even get started on their stubbornness. Ask a dachshund to do something they don't want to, and you'll be met with a defiant stare that says, "You're not the boss of me." These dogs have mastered the art of passive resistance. They'll lie down mid-walk, refuse to budge, and look at you like, "You carry me now, peasant." But it's their mischievous streak that steals the show. Leave a plate of food unattended, and your dachshund will transform into a stealthy ninja, snatching a bite before you even blink. Yet no matter how much trouble they cause, their soulful eyes and cheeky grins make it impossible to stay mad.

Fact 5: Dachshunds Have a Royal Pedigree

Queen Victoria, one of history's most famous dog lovers, was a proud dachshund owner.

She adored these quirky little dogs and helped popularize the breed in England. The Queen reportedly said, "Nothing will turn a man's home into a castle more quickly and effectively than a dachshund."

And she wasn't wrong. Dachshunds bring a regal flair to any household, strutting around like they own the place (because, let's face it, they do). They have an uncanny ability to charm everyone they meet, whether it's with their goofy antics or their affectionate cuddles.

Modern dachshunds might not live in castles, but they still expect royal treatment. From cozy beds to gourmet treats, these dogs demand the best—and their owners happily oblige. After all, when you have a sausage dog, you're not just a pet owner. You're a loyal subject to a tiny, furry monarch.

Fact 6: Dachshunds Are Natural Born "Spy Dogs"

Dachshunds are not only adorable—they're secretly spies in disguise. These clever little dogs are known for their ability to sneak around undetected. Whether it's a piece of cheese left unattended or your favorite pair of socks mysteriously disappearing, dachshunds are like tiny burglars with fur coats. They'll slink around with a stealthy determination, and before you even realize it, they've managed to steal your lunch—or your heart.

Their "spy-like" behavior is part of their natural instincts. As hunting dogs, dachshunds were bred to be quick, quiet, and elusive. These traits have translated into modern times, where they can sneak past you with the precision of a cat burglar.

But it's not all stealth and sneaky moves. Dachshunds also have a tendency to follow their humans everywhere, ensuring they don't miss a single moment of action. Whether you're walking into another room or taking a shower, a dachshund is always there, keeping watch like a loyal (and very cute) secret agent.

Fact 7: Their Legs Might Be Short, But Their Dreams Are Big

Dachshunds have some of the shortest legs in the dog world, but what they lack in stature, they make up for in confidence. These dogs think they're big dogs trapped in small bodies. They'll bark at anything that moves—whether it's a passing squirrel, a leaf blowing by, or a dog 10 times their size.

What's even more impressive is their complete disregard for their short legs. You'd think a dog with such a low center of gravity might be a little more cautious, but not the dachshund. These tiny warriors will attempt to scale anything that's even remotely climbable. From couches to kitchen counters, if they see an opportunity to assert their dominance (or snag a snack), they'll go for it with all their might.

And it's not just physical feats. Dachshunds have a big heart and an even bigger personality. They may be small in size, but they have the confidence of a lion. Their bravery and sassy attitude make them lovable and endlessly entertaining.

Fact 8: Dachshunds Are Masters of the Guilt Trip

If there's one thing dachshunds excel at, it's giving you the look. You know the one—the big, soulful eyes that seem to say, "I'm heartbroken. How could you do this to me?" Whether it's leaving them home alone for a few hours or not sharing your pizza, dachshunds are experts at making you feel guilty for every little thing.

They've perfected the art of the dramatic sigh. If you try to walk away from them, they'll stare at you like you've just betrayed them for life. If they don't get what they want, they'll give you a sad whine, as if they've never experienced a happy moment in their entire life.

And don't even try to ignore them. Their sad puppy eyes will haunt your dreams until you give in. Before you know it, you'll be back on the couch with your dachshund snuggled in your lap, sharing your snack—and feeling like you're the best pet parent in the world (because, let's face it, they know how to work their charm).

Fact 9: Their Dachshund "Bark" Sounds Like a Squeaky Toy

Dachshunds are often known for their signature bark, which, to be fair, sounds more like a squeaky toy than a dog's bark. This high-pitched, often startling yelp is both hilarious and surprisingly effective. When they bark, it's as if they're trying to make sure the entire neighborhood knows their opinion on the matter—whether it's a passing car, a distant bird, or an unfamiliar noise.

The sound of a dachshund barking is so unique that it has led many owners to joke that their dogs are secretly made of rubber and springs. Imagine being on a Zoom call when your dachshund suddenly decides to bark at a passing squirrel—it's like a car alarm going off in the background, but much more adorable.

What's even funnier is that while their bark may sound tough, dachshunds are often scaredy-cats when it comes to loud noises, like thunderstorms or fireworks. They'll curl up in your lap as if trying to become one with your body, clearly convinced that the world is ending. It's hard to take them seriously when they're shaking in fear, but that's part of their charm.

Fact 10: Dachshunds Were Popular Among Celebrities and Artists

The dachshund's charm extends far beyond the average household. Throughout history, these dogs have been beloved by some of the most influential figures in culture, art, and entertainment. For example, famous artist Frida Kahlo had a dachshund named Fulang-Chang, who was often seen in her paintings. Similarly, John F. Kennedy and his wife Jacqueline had a dachshund named Charlie, who was known for his charming presence at the White House.

But it's not just famous people who love dachshunds. The breed has appeared in countless art pieces, from sculptures to paintings, and has even been immortalized in pop culture. The famous Peanuts comic strip by Charles Schulz featured a dachshund named Spike, who added a bit of canine wisdom and humor to the strip. So, next time you see a dachshund walking down the street, remember that you're looking at a dog with royal history and an impressive pedigree—not just a cute face and short legs. With their long history of cultural influence, dachshunds are the true rockstars of the dog world.

Fact 11: Dachshunds Are Fearless—Even When They Shouldn't Be

One of the most endearing qualities of dachshunds is their absolute lack of concern for size. Despite being small and low to the ground, they have the courage of much larger dogs, and they're not afraid to show it. In fact, many dachshunds believe they're the toughest dogs on the block—and they're willing to prove it, even if it means picking a fight with something 10 times their size.

Take, for example, their encounters with larger dogs. While a bigger dog might be content to observe a situation, the dachshund is already halfway toward the perceived threat, barking furiously, and ready to square off. Whether it's a full-grown labrador or even a German shepherd, your dachshund will happily charge at them like they're ready to win the doggy UFC championship. Of course, the moment the big dog responds with a playful wag or a simple sniff, your dachshund will promptly back off—but not without putting up a valiant effort first.

This bravery isn't limited to just dog encounters either. Dachshunds will stand up to any challenge, whether it's a noisy vacuum cleaner or an overly large (but still harmless) lawnmower. They'll bark and jump in front of it, thinking they're the protectors of the household, ensuring that the "danger" knows it's not welcome in their kingdom.

Fact 12: Dachshunds Are Surprisingly Great Swimmers

When you think of dachshunds, the image that comes to mind isn't likely that of a water-loving retriever or a graceful swimmer. But surprisingly, these little wiener dogs are great swimmers—thanks to their long bodies, powerful legs, and natural curiosity.

Despite their short legs, dachshunds can paddle their way across a lake, pool, or any other body of water that they're brave enough to enter. Their instinct to swim may be traced back to their history as hunting dogs. Originally bred in Germany to burrow into badger holes, dachshunds had to navigate through rivers and ponds to track down their prey. This ability to swim, combined with their fearless nature, makes them surprisingly proficient in water. However, like many things with dachshunds, it's a love-hate relationship. Some dachshunds, while capable swimmers, may need a little encouragement to get their paws wet. Others might enthusiastically dive into the water, not realizing they might need a lifejacket due to their shorter stature. If your dachshund doesn't immediately fall in love with swimming, don't worry—it's just part of their quirky personality. Either way, it's always fun to see them trying to figure out the water world!

Fact 13: Their Ears Have a Mind of Their Own

Dachshund ears are one of their most charming features, but did you know these ears have a life of their own? Long, floppy, and often comically oversized for their bodies, dachshund ears seem to have a mind of their own. They move with the speed of sound, perking up at the slightest noise, or flopping down when they're relaxed—giving your dachshund the most expressive and endearing look. However, there's more to these floppy ears than just cuteness. Their large ears serve an important purpose. Dachshunds have an excellent sense of hearing, and their ears help them detect even the faintest of sounds. Whether it's the rustling of a squirrel in the bushes or the sound of a snack bag opening, those ears are always on high alert. Dachshunds have also mastered the art of using their ears to communicate their mood. When they're excited, their ears are perked up, and they may even wag them like a tail. When they're confused or curious, their ears might move independently of each other, giving them a look of intense concentration. And when they're not interested in something (like a bath), their ears will droop sadly, as if to say, "I don't care, but I'll pretend I do."

Fact 14: Dachshunds Have an Ancient Ancestry That Dates Back to Ancient Egypt

You may not have known it, but dachshunds have some serious royal and ancient credentials. While the breed as we know it today emerged in Germany, their ancestors can be traced all the way back to Ancient Egypt, where short-legged dogs resembling the dachshund were revered as companions by pharaohs and royalty.

In fact, one of the earliest representations of a dog resembling the dachshund appears in Egyptian art, where a small, elongated dog is seen hunting with its owner. These early "dachshund-like" dogs were believed to have been bred for their ability to hunt small game like rabbits and other prey, using their agility and cleverness to squeeze into tight spaces. Fast forward several centuries, and the dachshund's role in history has remained largely the same. They were prized by German hunters for their ability to dig into badger dens, and they were even featured in paintings and sculptures by renowned artists in Europe. But regardless of whether they were chasing small game in ancient Egypt or lounging on modern-day sofas, dachshunds have always been cherished companions.

Fact 15: Their Love for Sunbathing Makes Them Part-Time Cats

If you've ever caught your dachshund basking in the sun, soaking up those warm rays, you may have noticed that your little dog seems more like a cat than a dog. Dachshunds are notorious for their love of sunbathing. Just like cats, they can often be found sprawled out in the sunniest spot of the house, eyes half-closed in complete relaxation.

This behavior is rooted in their ancestors' hunting habits. Dachshunds were originally bred to hunt in the chilly forests of Germany, and they would often rest in the sun to warm up after a long day of burrowing. Today, even though they no longer need to hunt, dachshunds still enjoy finding the perfect patch of sunlight to nap in.

If you want to make your dachshund's day, simply open a window on a sunny day, and watch them flop down in front of it, grinning like they've just discovered the best secret spot in the house. Dachshunds are natural sun worshippers, and they embrace it with the same enthusiasm that cats do—making them honorary felines in your home.

Fact 16: Dachshunds Are Definitely Not the "Lap Dog" You Think They Are

When most people picture a lap dog, they imagine a small, calm dog that cuddles contentedly, curling up in your lap for hours of quiet snuggling. But don't expect a dachshund to be the stereotypical lap dog you might imagine! While these little sausages love attention, they're not quite as "chill" as you'd think.

Dachshunds are active and curious little creatures that need constant engagement. Rather than simply lounging in your lap for a long nap, they may hop up and down, wanting to explore, or demand that you play with them. If you're sitting down on the couch, be prepared for them to climb into your lap—not to stay still, but to ensure you're always aware of their presence. They might settle down, but only when they've thoroughly scoped out the situation.

While they may enjoy being close to you, don't be fooled into thinking they'll stay put for long. These dogs have a relentless curiosity and a need for action. Whether it's peeking out of the window, checking out new sounds, or playfully biting your fingers (because they're trying to tell you something), your lap is just a temporary stop on their adventure journey. Dachshunds are truly a lap dog with a twist—constantly in motion and demanding attention when you least expect it.

Fact 17: Dachshunds Have Their Own "Quirky" Personality Traits

Dachshunds are known for their big personalities packed into small bodies. These dogs have a distinct character and attitude that make them stand out from other breeds. Not only are they courageous, but they also possess a certain quirky charm that makes them absolutely lovable.

First of all, dachshunds can be stubborn. While they are intelligent and quick to learn, they tend to be independent thinkers. If they don't want to do something, they'll let you know. Whether it's refusing to come when called or stubbornly ignoring a command they've learned a hundred times, dachshunds often do what they want, and that's that.

But their quirkiness doesn't stop there. Dachshunds can also be incredibly affectionate, following you around and showering you with love in their own unique ways. They might want to be right next to you all day long, or they could surprise you by jumping on your lap and demanding cuddles out of nowhere. Their way of showing affection can seem a bit odd—whether it's licking your hand, pawing at your face, or snuggling into your armpit—but it's all part of their distinctive charm.

They may be a bit stubborn and independent, but once you understand their personality, you'll find that their quirks make them irresistible.

Fact 18: Dachshunds Have an Incredible Sense of Smell—But They Can't Be Trusted With Snacks

If you've ever had a dachshund and tried to eat anything within their reach, you know that they have an extraordinary sense of smell. Their noses are so sharp they can detect the faintest scent from miles away, which makes them excellent hunters. This olfactory superpower is a big part of their history as badger hunters in Germany, as their keen noses helped them track down animals in underground dens.

But here's the funny thing: While dachshunds can sniff out the tiniest morsel of food from a mile away, they can't always be trusted when it comes to "sharing" their findings. They will definitely try to steal your snacks, even if it means sitting quietly next to you, staring at your food with an intensity that would make even the most stoic person uncomfortable.

If you're having a snack and a dachshund is nearby, don't be surprised if you look away for a second only to find that they've snuck up and taken a bite. They've learned that their charming eyes and innocent face can get them out of many tricky situations, so they'll use these skills to beg for food. Of course, they won't hesitate to take it without asking either.

Fact 19: They Were Born to Dig—But Only When You're Watching

Dachshunds are digging enthusiasts. Thanks to their history as burrowing badger hunters, these dogs have a natural instinct to dig. Whether it's dirt, sand, or even your favorite cozy blanket, nothing is safe from their digging paws. You might find them scratching at the couch, fluffing up their beds, or enthusiastically digging in the garden (much to your dismay).

The funny thing about this digging habit is that dachshunds are selective about when they dig. For instance, while they're perfectly capable of digging up the entire backyard when left unsupervised, they'll often start digging only when you're in the room to see it. It's as if they want to show off their skills, as though they're saying, "Look, I could be digging up the whole yard, but I'll settle for this pillow right here."

If your dachshund gets bored or excited, don't be surprised if they start making a "digging circle" in their bed. They'll do this little spin, scratching at the fabric like they're digging for treasure. It's all part of their playful, adventurous spirit—and a bit of a hassle when you're trying to relax!

Fact 20: Dachshunds Are Surprisingly Great Athletes

While dachshunds may not look like traditional athletes, they're actually quite the sports enthusiasts. Their love for running and jumping often surprises first-time owners. These tiny dogs may have short legs, but they've got tons of energy packed into their little frames. Dachshunds love a good sprint and can keep up with larger dogs when it comes to chasing balls, playing in the yard, or just running around like a blur of fur. Their small, muscular bodies and quick reflexes make them excellent in short bursts of action. If you've ever thrown a ball for a dachshund, you might have noticed that they can run at surprisingly high speeds for such short dogs.

But the fun doesn't stop at running. Dachshunds love playing games like fetch, and some owners even train them to do agility courses, where they excel at weaving through poles and jumping over obstacles. Despite their small size, they're determined to keep up with the big dogs, and their natural athleticism is always a sight to see.

Fact 21: Dachshunds Are Known for Their "Dachshund Dash"

Dachshunds have a peculiar running style that has earned them the nickname of "Dachshund Dash." While they may not be the fastest dogs on the block, their adorable, slightly comical waddle and determined expressions while running are enough to make anyone laugh. The short legs and long bodies of a dachshund give them a distinct, almost hopping, gait when they're trying to sprint. Their "Dachshund Dash" is a sight to behold, and no one can deny how cute they look while they're in full sprint mode. The little legs work overtime as they try to keep up with larger dogs, and sometimes their determination can result in them zooming around in a zigzag pattern, making their movements even more hilarious.

This dash is often seen when dachshunds get excited—whether it's a game of fetch, the doorbell ringing, or just the joy of running through a wide-open space. So if you ever see a dachshund dashing around like a blur of energy, know that they're just indulging in their favorite pastime. It's a part of their playful spirit that makes them irresistible.

Fact 22: Dachshunds Have a Strong "Bark"

Despite their small size, dachshunds are notorious for their big bark. These little dogs often sound like they're much larger than they actually are, surprising anyone who hasn't heard them before. With a loud, deep bark, a dachshund can alert you to anything from an approaching squirrel to a mailman at the door. What's more surprising is that dachshunds can actually be quite protective of their family, and their bark serves as a warning to any potential threats. While they may be tiny in size, they certainly don't act like it when it comes to protecting their territory. In fact, some dachshunds can even take on dogs several times their size when they feel their home is threatened.

This tenacity, combined with their loud bark, often gives dachshunds a reputation for being fearless. But it also means that dachshund owners should be prepared for the noise when their pups decide it's time to alert the whole neighborhood about something they deem important.

Fact 23: Dachshunds Are the Best "Nap Buddies"

Dachshunds may be energetic, but they also have a knack for turning into professional nappers. Their small size and comfortable, fluffy bodies make them ideal for cozying up on a bed, couch, or blanket for a long, luxurious nap. You may even find that your dachshund is more skilled at finding the perfect napping spot than you are! When dachshunds aren't chasing after toys or running around, they can easily transition into the best napping companions. They love curling up in tight, warm spots where they can feel safe and secure. If you're ever having a lazy afternoon and you're looking for someone to join you in a nap, a dachshund is likely to be the perfect snuggle buddy.

But don't expect them to stay napping for too long. Dachshunds are known to alternate between bursts of energy and long snooze sessions. It's not uncommon to see a dachshund suddenly spring into action, just to end up back in a curled-up position within minutes. They're true professionals when it comes to balancing playtime with rest.

Fact 24: Dachshunds Can Be Very Vocal About Their Wants

It's no secret that dachshunds have a lot to say, and they're not shy about it. They've mastered the art of vocalization to let you know exactly what they want. Whether it's food, attention, or a play session, a dachshund will make sure their voice is heard.

They use a variety of sounds to communicate, including barking, whining, and even the occasional howl. If a dachshund is feeling a little neglected, they may whine softly to remind you that it's time for some love and affection. If they're hungry or want a treat, they won't hesitate to make sure you know it—sometimes with a bit of a dramatic flair.

In fact, many dachshund owners find that their dogs have distinct ways of "talking" to them. Some dachshunds have even been known to bark in response to certain words or sounds. They may have a way of letting you know when it's time for a walk, when they're bored, or when they need a bathroom break, all with their vocal talents.

Fact 25: Dachshunds Have a Unique Sense of Humor

Dachshunds have a playful, often mischievous side, which means they also have an exceptional sense of humor. They love to entertain and often do so by acting out, making you laugh with their funny antics. Whether it's running around with a toy, trying to squeeze into a space that's clearly too small for them, or even pulling a funny face, these dogs know how to get a good laugh.

Their humor is often a mix of cute and clever. Dachshunds love to get attention and will do just about anything to make you smile. They have a certain charm that comes from their funny facial expressions, their endearing movements, and their playful personality. You may find them rolling around on the floor, playing "hide and seek," or giving you a look that could only be described as pure comedic timing.

Their goofy behavior is one of the things that makes them so lovable, and their unique sense of humor is something you can never quite predict. So if you ever need a good laugh, just spend a little time with a dachshund. You'll be surprised at how these little dogs can turn any moment into a joyful, funny experience.

Fact 26: Dachshunds Have a Rich History as Hunters and Royal Companions

Dachshunds didn't just evolve into adorable pets—these little dogs have a storied past as brave hunters. Originally bred in Germany during the 17th century, dachshunds were specifically developed to dig into burrows and hunt badgers. Their long bodies and short legs were ideal for squeezing into tight spaces to chase down prey. In fact, their name, "Dachshund," literally translates to "badger dog" in German (from "Dachs" for badger and "Hund" for dog).

But despite their humble, hardworking beginnings as fierce hunters, dachshunds have also enjoyed periods of royal recognition. Throughout history, they were favored by royalty and aristocracy. The famous Austrian Empress Maria Theresa and King Frederick II of Prussia were both known for owning dachshunds, and they were often found by the sides of European nobles. These royal connections helped cement the breed's status as both a loyal working dog and a charming companion.

The contrast between their hunting roots and their pampered status among nobility just adds to the charm of these small but mighty dogs. From the fields of Germany to the grand courts of Europe, dachshunds have lived a life of both adventure and luxury.

Fact 27: Dachshunds Have Big Dog Energy in a Small Dog's Body

Dachshunds may be tiny, but they sure have a lot of "big dog" energy packed into their small bodies. These dogs don't know their size—they believe they're just as powerful and capable as any large dog around. Whether it's standing their ground against much bigger dogs or charging ahead in a game of fetch, dachshunds have no fear when it comes to taking on the world. Their bold personalities can often surprise people who aren't familiar with the breed. While they may be small enough to fit on your lap, dachshunds have a loud, confident presence that's impossible to ignore. They are often unapologetically stubborn, and their determination and courage sometimes make them act far larger than they actually are. Dachshunds' bravery often leads to hilarious situations, like when they try to challenge a larger dog at the park, or when they bark ferociously at a doorbell, as if they're guarding the castle. It's this undeniable "big dog" energy that makes them such lovable, funny companions.

Fact 28: Dachshunds Are Known for Their 'Dachshund Dance'

Ever seen a dachshund get excited and break out into what can only be described as a "Dachshund Dance"? These little dogs are known for their quirky, energetic way of expressing joy when they're happy or excited. When a dachshund is particularly eager or excited, they often perform an adorable little dance—a series of quick hops, spins, and wiggling movements that show just how thrilled they are.

The dance is usually seen when you come home after being away, when it's time for their walk, or when they see something they're excited about (like a treat or a toy). Their short legs make the dance even more endearing, as they hop around with all their might, eager to share their excitement. It's a funny little display of happiness that's hard to resist, and it's just one of the many charming traits that make dachshunds so beloved.

You'll quickly learn that the "Dachshund Dance" isn't just cute—it's also contagious. Once your dachshund starts performing, you might find yourself laughing so hard that you want to join in!

Fact 29: Dachshunds Are Surprisingly Good at Digging—and Not Just in the Garden

Dachshunds come from a long line of burrowers, and that instinct to dig runs deep. Originally bred to dig out badgers from their dens, they've kept this talent alive. If you have a garden, you may notice that your dachshund has a tendency to dig up your flowers or favorite plants. But it's not just your garden that's at risk.

Dachshunds can dig up anything they find interesting, from their own bedding to your favorite couch cushion. You might catch them digging in the middle of your living room, trying to make a perfect little "nest." The digging behavior is especially common when they're feeling bored or anxious, as it helps them release pent-up energy and create a space they can claim as their own. Interestingly, dachshunds also dig when they want your attention. You might find them digging around your feet when you're sitting, demanding that you focus on them instead of whatever you're doing. This quirky behavior adds to their charming, stubborn nature. They may look sweet, but they've got a mind of their own and will do what it takes to make sure you know it!

Fact 30: Dachshunds Can Be Quite the "Drama Queens"

Dachshunds are known to be a bit dramatic at times, and this dramatic flair is one of their funniest and most endearing qualities. Whether it's giving you a dramatic stare when they're not getting their way or acting as if they've suffered the greatest of injustices, dachshunds know how to create a scene.

When a dachshund is upset (whether they're being left out of the action, not getting a treat, or just not feeling like doing something), they may resort to dramatic behavior. They'll let out exaggerated sighs, flop down dramatically on the floor, or even "storm off" to a corner as if they've been wronged. Sometimes, they'll whine or give you the "puppy dog eyes" in the most theatrical way possible, knowing full well that you'll be moved by their performance.

This tendency toward dramatics makes them great at getting attention, but it also means that dachshunds have the potential to be the center of the show. And when they do perform, it's impossible not to smile at their over-the-top antics.

Fact 31: Dachshunds Are a Hit at Dog Parks—But Only If They're the "Boss"

Dachshunds might be small, but they're not afraid to show their dominance when they're at the dog park. In fact, they often act like they're the "alpha" of the park, no matter how much bigger the other dogs are. While they're often friendly and social with other dogs, dachshunds also have a natural instinct to assert themselves. If a dachshund thinks another dog is getting too close to their personal space or trying to take over their favorite toy, they'll let the intruder know who's in charge. They may stand their ground, bark loudly, or even give a little nudge to make sure the other dog knows who the real boss is. It's not uncommon to see a dachshund taking charge, even if they're surrounded by dogs that are much larger than they are.

But their dog park dominance doesn't mean they don't know how to socialize. They're just as likely to get along with the other dogs—once they've established that they're the leader of the pack.

Fact 32: Dachshunds Have an Incredible Sense of Smell

Dachshunds were originally bred as hunting dogs, specifically for tracking down and hunting small animals like badgers. And though they may now be cuddled up on your couch, they still retain that impressive sense of smell that made them exceptional hunters. Their noses are finely tuned to detect even the faintest of scents, which makes them skilled at tracking down everything from a hidden treat to the smell of their favorite human.

Their sense of smell is so powerful that, according to some studies, dachshunds can distinguish between different odors more effectively than some larger hunting breeds. This trait can be both helpful and hilarious. For example, if you think you've hidden a snack somewhere safe, you'll soon find out that your dachshund can sniff it out in seconds.

Even though they're small in stature, dachshunds' noses are an important part of their identity and a testament to their hunting roots. They have an amazing ability to detect scents in complex environments, which helps explain their sometimes obsessive behavior of sniffing around the house, yard, or even in the most unlikely of places. They're truly born to sniff and track!

Fact 33: Dachshunds Are the Masters of the "Guilty Face"

If you've ever caught your dachshund doing something they shouldn't—like chewing on a shoe or sneaking a snack from the kitchen—you've likely witnessed what we can only call a "guilty face." Dachshunds have this uncanny ability to look completely guilty, even when they haven't been caught in the act. With those large, expressive eyes and a downward turn of the mouth, it's as if they know exactly what they've done wrong.

The funny part? Sometimes they'll give you that look even if you haven't seen them do anything wrong! It's almost as if they've learned the power of a guilty expression and are using it to manipulate you into feeling bad for them. Some owners believe their dachshund's "guilty face" is a combination of their awareness of your disapproval and their natural ability to convey emotion through body language.

It's a trait that's both hilarious and endearing—no matter how many times they break the rules, you can't help but laugh when they give you that adorable, apologetic stare. You'll be left wondering if they really do feel guilty—or if they're just playing the system!

Fact 34: Dachshunds Have a Love Affair with Warmth

If there's one thing most dachshunds agree on, it's that they love being warm and cozy. Whether it's burrowing under a pile of blankets or nestling up in a sunny spot on the floor, dachshunds are notorious for seeking out warmth at all costs. This isn't just a preference; it's also tied to their history. As hunters, dachshunds were used to working in cool, underground spaces where the temperature was relatively constant. So, after a long day of hunting badgers or rabbits, they'd naturally retreat to warm, comfortable spots to rest. This love for warmth was likely bred into them, as their smaller size and long bodies make it easier for them to lose heat quickly.

This obsession with warmth can lead to some truly funny moments. You might catch your dachshund trying to sneak into a laundry basket full of warm clothes or curling up in your shoes just because they're the warmest place they can find. On chilly days, they'll often seek out a sunny window or even curl up near a heater, never wanting to miss a chance to bask in the glow of warmth.

Fact 35: Dachshunds Are Natural Burrowers—Watch Out for Your Bed

As descendants of burrowing dogs used to chase down badgers and other small prey, dachshunds have an innate need to dig and burrow. This doesn't just apply to the outdoors; many dachshunds can't resist digging in your bed, blankets, or couch cushions. It's their way of creating a "den," which is an instinct that dates back to their wild ancestors.

Sometimes, their digging can get a little out of hand. You might walk into a room to find that your dachshund has dug a hole in your comforter or turned your pillows into a shredded mess. It's all part of their nature, but it can be quite comical to witness. You can almost imagine them thinking, "If I dig deep enough, I'll find a treasure!"

What's even funnier is when they dig and then get frustrated because they can't seem to make the perfect hole. They'll scratch at the bed with all their might, only to flop down dramatically once they realize they've made no progress. It's a hilarious mix of stubbornness and instinct!

Fact 36: Dachshunds Have a Serious Love for Car Rides—They're Born Travelers

Dachshunds aren't just content with being your homebody companion; they love a good car ride. Whether it's a short trip to the vet or a long road trip, dachshunds are often thrilled by the motion of the car. Their curiosity and excitement are almost palpable when you start the engine, and they'll eagerly jump into the car, wagging their tails and looking out the window, as if they're about to embark on an adventure.

Interestingly, dachshunds were originally bred to be both brave hunters and fearless travelers. In their earlier days, they would travel with their owners on long journeys through the German countryside, assisting with hunting and being companions along the way. Today, dachshunds still carry this traveling spirit with them, whether it's a car ride to the park or a cross-country trip to visit family.

Their love for car rides makes them the perfect travel companion. In fact, many dachshund owners swear their pets are better behaved on road trips than some humans! Just make sure you've got a comfy spot for them to settle into—your dachshund will let you know if they're not thrilled with their seating arrangement!

Fact 37: Dachshunds Can Be Quite the Foodies

Dachshunds might be small, but their appetites are legendary. These little dogs love food, and they love to eat. As a breed that was originally used for hunting, dachshunds developed a keen appreciation for any form of sustenance. It's no wonder they can sniff out a snack from miles away!

Their food-driven nature can lead to some hilarious and sometimes mischievous behavior. A dachshund might leap to the counter to steal a snack when no one's looking or give you their most convincing "feed me" eyes until you can't resist giving them a treat.

But it's not just any food that piques their interest. Dachshunds are known to have a refined palate and will often turn their noses up at low-quality treats in favor of something more delicious. They're true foodies, and you might find them "sampling" everything from your sandwich to the crumbs under the dinner table.

It's this love for food that also makes them incredibly trainable when it comes to food-related commands. You can bet your dachshund will do just about anything for a bite of their favorite treat!

Fact 38: Dachshunds Have a Sense of Humor

Dachshunds are not only adorable but also surprisingly funny. Their quirky, independent nature and intelligence often lead them to develop their own sense of humor. Whether they're amusing themselves by running in circles for no apparent reason or making you laugh with their goofy antics, dachshunds are born entertainers. One of their favorite ways to be funny is through exaggerated behaviors. For example, they may suddenly freeze and stare intently at a spot on the wall for no apparent reason, only to start barking and running around as if they've discovered some mysterious creature. They might also put on their best "suspicious" look, tilting their heads at an angle while observing everything around them as though they're solving a complex mystery. Their humor can also show in their playfulness, like when they do something unexpectedly silly, such as jumping straight up in the air or chasing their own tail. It's as though they understand the power of laughter and use it to charm everyone around them. Their antics never seem to get old, and it's no surprise that dachshunds are known for brightening up their owners' days with laughter.

Fact 39: Dachshunds Love to Be the Center of Attention

If there's one thing dachshunds love more than food and cuddles, it's attention. These little dogs have an undeniable charm and are experts at getting all eyes on them. Their small size combined with their bold personalities makes them natural attention seekers. Whether it's through their unique vocalizations, their adorable looks, or their clever antics, dachshunds always find ways to become the center of any room.

It's not uncommon for a dachshund to demand attention in hilarious ways. They might nudge your hand until you pet them, give you their "sad" eyes when you're not paying enough attention, or even jump into your lap with dramatic flair. If there's something going on—whether it's a family gathering, a dinner party, or even just a quiet evening—they will insist on being the focus.

In fact, some dachshunds are so skilled at attracting attention that they will even compete with other pets in the household for their share of love. They've got a competitive streak when it comes to affection, and their small size doesn't stop them from getting right in the middle of the action.

Fact 40: Dachshunds Can Be Excellent Therapy Dogs

While they might be tiny, dachshunds have hearts that are just as big as their personalities. Many dachshunds have an innate ability to provide comfort and companionship, making them excellent therapy dogs. Their empathetic nature and deep bond with their owners mean that they often intuitively know when someone needs comfort. Whether it's cuddling up on the couch with you during a tough day or offering a warm paw during stressful moments, dachshunds are great at providing emotional support.

What makes them even more suited to therapy work is their intelligence and willingness to learn. Dachshunds enjoy having a job to do, and many owners have trained their dachshunds to offer support in a variety of situations. Whether it's visiting hospitals, nursing homes, or simply being a loving companion at home, these little dogs are known to make an impact.

Their calm demeanor and affectionate nature make them the perfect companion for those in need of emotional support. Their small size and big heart are a combination that brings comfort to many, proving that sometimes the best therapists come in small, furry packages.

Fact 41: Dachshunds Love to Dig—It's in Their DNA

You may have caught your dachshund digging in the garden, in the couch cushions, or even under the bed covers. This behavior is deeply rooted in their DNA as a result of their history as hunters and burrowers. Dachshunds were originally bred to dig out badgers from their burrows, so their digging instinct is incredibly strong.

When a dachshund digs, they are essentially "following their instincts" to create a burrow or den—something they would have done in the wild for safety and comfort. While this behavior might be amusing when they dig in your blanket pile, it can become a little frustrating when they start digging up your flower bed.

Interestingly, dachshunds will often dig in circles, which is another quirky trait passed down from their burrowing ancestors. They may dig in the grass, bedding, or even your shoes, trying to create the perfect nest. It's their way of making themselves comfortable, and it's part of their charming, mischievous personality.

While this digging is natural, some dachshunds may take it to extremes, digging deep enough to uncover hidden treasures (or the occasional buried snack). And even if it's not always convenient for you, it's undeniably a part of their adorable nature.

Fact 42: Dachshunds Are Surprisingly Agile for Their Size

Though dachshunds may look like little sausages on legs, they're actually quite agile. Their long bodies and short legs might suggest otherwise, but these dogs can be surprisingly fast and nimble when they need to be.

As hunters, dachshunds were bred to navigate tunnels and burrows, so they developed strong muscles in their legs that help them dig, sprint, and twist with impressive agility. This agility comes in handy in many situations—whether it's chasing after a favorite toy or darting around the house in a game of fetch.

In fact, many dachshund owners are often amazed at their dog's ability to jump onto furniture, crawl through tight spaces, and even dart across a room in an instant. Their long, low bodies may look awkward, but they can outmaneuver you in a blink of an eye when they decide to show off their athleticism. Their agility is especially important when it comes to hunting, as dachshunds needed to move quickly and nimbly in pursuit of their prey. So, if you think dachshunds are just little lap dogs with no athletic ability, think again—these dogs have got some serious moves!

Fact 43: Dachshunds Are Actually Very Protective of Their Family

Though dachshunds are small, they're often fiercely protective of their family. Despite their size, many dachshunds take their role as "guard dogs" very seriously. They're not afraid to bark at strangers, and they often show an exaggerated reaction when they feel their family is in danger—or even when something feels "off" in their environment.

This protective nature can be quite humorous, as dachshunds tend to bark and alert you to things that are not actually threats, such as the mailman, the neighbor's cat, or even a leaf blowing by. But their over-the-top reactions prove just how much they care for their family. What's more surprising is that their protective instincts don't just apply to their human family members. Many dachshunds will also stand guard over their fellow pets in the household, showing that their loyalty extends beyond just the humans they love. They may act small, but they have a big heart when it comes to looking after their loved ones.

Fact 44: Dachshunds Have a Tendency to Get "The Zoomies"

If you've ever seen a dachshund burst out of nowhere, running in circles, zigzagging through the house, and generally acting like a maniac, you're not alone. This hilarious phenomenon is called "the zoomies," and it's something almost all dachshunds experience at least once in their lives.

Zoomies usually happen when a dachshund has a sudden burst of energy, often after a nap or a play session. You might find your dachshund running at full speed through the living room, launching themselves over furniture, or dashing from one end of the yard to the other in a flurry of energy. These little bursts of enthusiasm are part of a natural behavior, as dachshunds, like many dogs, are prone to moments of sudden excitement.

Interestingly, the zoomies seem to be a way for dachshunds to release pent-up energy. It's almost like they're letting out all the fun they've stored up throughout the day. Their short legs may give them an adorable, slightly awkward running style, but that doesn't stop them from dashing around with all the enthusiasm of a much larger dog.

Zoomies aren't always limited to running either—sometimes your dachshund might suddenly jump into the air, roll on the ground, or dart around the house with exaggerated moves. It's one of the most entertaining and comical things about them, and it never gets old!

Fact 45: Dachshunds Have a Huge Appetite (and a Big Personality to Match)

Dachshunds might be small, but their appetites can rival those of much larger breeds. They love food, and they're not shy about showing it! Whether it's mealtime or just a random snack, dachshunds are notorious for getting excited about food.

This love for food can sometimes lead to some amusing situations. For instance, if a dachshund is ever left alone with food on the counter, it might somehow find a way to climb up and steal it—even if that means using their little paws like a professional food thief! Their persistence can be both impressive and downright funny when they're on the hunt for snacks.

What's even more interesting is their tendency to have a strong personality around food. Dachshunds can be possessive about their meals, and they may even growl or act protective when someone comes too close to their bowl. This protective behavior is their way of ensuring that no one takes away their beloved food. Despite their small size, dachshunds will often try to get the biggest portion or the tastiest treat, displaying their bold and confident nature. Their love for food is just another example of their bigger-than-life personalities.

Fact 46: Dachshunds Have the Best "Sad Eyes" in the Dog World

There's no denying it—dachshunds are absolute masters of giving their owners those heart-melting "sad eyes." It's as if they have a special power to look directly into your soul and convince you to give them anything they want. Whether it's a treat, extra attention, or just a spot on the couch, their expressive eyes make it almost impossible to say no to them.

This trait is part of their deep connection with their owners. Dachshunds have an ability to convey emotions with just a glance, using their big, dark eyes to show longing, curiosity, or a sense of deep love. They've learned that humans respond to their "sad eyes," and they use it to their advantage, often getting pampered with extra goodies and affection.

While it's hard to resist their pleading gaze, it's also a source of comedy. You'll find yourself laughing at how dramatic they can be when they don't get exactly what they want. Whether they're gazing up at you from under the table or lying down with a dramatic sigh, their "sad eyes" never fail to entertain.

Fact 47: Dachshunds Are Surprisingly Vocal

Dachshunds may be small in size, but they've got some big voices. These dogs are known for being quite vocal and are often unafraid to express their thoughts with barks, howls, and whines.

If a dachshund hears something—whether it's the mailman at the door, a squirrel outside the window, or the sound of a treat bag rustling—they will let you know about it. Their barking is often loud, and it can seem disproportionate to their size, which makes it even more comical.

Some dachshunds are more talkative than others, but most will happily engage in a little "conversation" with their owners. They might bark when they're excited, when they want attention, or even just because they feel like it. Some dachshunds will even vocalize in response to their owners, making it seem like they're having a back-and-forth exchange.

Interestingly, dachshunds don't just bark for no reason. They've been bred to be alert hunters, so they'll bark to alert you of any perceived danger, whether it's a real threat or just something they find suspicious. So, if you hear your dachshund barking, you know they're trying to keep you safe—or simply asking for attention!

Fact 48: Dachshunds Are "Lap Dogs" in Disguise

Though dachshunds have a reputation for being independent and energetic, they also have a surprising love for cuddling. Their small size and affectionate nature make them natural lap dogs, and many dachshund owners will attest to the fact that their little dog often insists on sitting in their lap for long stretches of time.

What's funny is that dachshunds often have no idea that they're not supposed to be on your lap, especially when there's clearly no room left. They will wedge themselves in, curl up as if they belong there, and look up at you with those irresistible eyes as if to say, "I'm your lap dog now."

This desire for lap time often comes at the most inconvenient moments—like when you're trying to work, eat, or even stretch your legs. But, despite their timing, their love for closeness is undeniable. They'll snuggle up with you on the couch or under the blankets, sharing warmth and affection. And once they're in your lap, they expect to stay there for as long as they like, completely content in their little space.

Fact 49: Dachshunds Have an Incredible Sense of Smell

Dachshunds may be small, but their noses are incredibly powerful. As hunting dogs, they were bred to track scents, and they still possess an extraordinary sense of smell.

Their keen olfactory abilities allow them to detect scents from a great distance, and they can easily follow a trail no matter how faint. This is why dachshunds often get distracted by new smells during walks—whether it's a fellow dog's scent, a tasty treat, or even just a new smell in the grass.

Their scent-tracking abilities are also why they make excellent hunting dogs. Dachshunds can follow the scent of their prey through tunnels, around obstacles, and in the most challenging environments. Their strong noses and determination make them fearless when it comes to sniffing out what they're after.

For dachshund owners, this sense of smell means that their dog might get a little obsessed with a new scent, often leading to adorable (and sometimes funny) behavior as they investigate and explore.

Fact 50: Dachshunds Are Fearless (Even When They Shouldn't Be)

Dachshunds might be small in stature, but their bravery is unmatched—sometimes to a hilariously dangerous degree! Despite their size, dachshunds have the heart of a lion and a fearless attitude that often gets them into comical situations.

Originally bred to hunt badgers, dachshunds were designed to dive into burrows and confront much larger animals. Their boldness still shines through today, and they often have a "big dog" attitude, especially when they believe they are protecting their family. It's not uncommon for a dachshund to bark fiercely at a dog many times its size or to approach an unfamiliar situation with a sense of complete invincibility.

One of the funniest things about their bravery is how it plays out in everyday life. Dachshunds will stand their ground, even if the "enemy" is something absurd, like a vacuum cleaner, a broom, or even a slightly larger dog at the park. Their small stature doesn't faze them in the slightest. You might even witness them charging full speed toward an object twice their size without any hesitation, only to realize that they're maybe in over their heads.

This fearless attitude is part of their charm. They'll take on the world, no matter how big it is, and they will never back down. It's this spunky attitude that makes dachshunds such lovable and entertaining companions. They truly believe they're the biggest dog in the room, even if everyone else knows better.

Fact 51: The Dachshund's Hidden Talent – Comedy Shows

Dachshunds are the accidental comedians of the dog world. Everything they do seems to be wrapped in an element of humor. Whether it's their clumsy tumbles while chasing a ball or their overly dramatic sighs when you won't share your dinner, dachshunds are natural entertainers.

Owners often find themselves laughing uncontrollably at their antics, even when they're trying to discipline them. Imagine this: your sausage dog gets caught red-pawed digging up your prized flower bed. They freeze, slowly tilt their head, and give you the classic "Who, me?" look. How can you stay mad at that?

But their comedic timing doesn't stop at their expressions. Dachshunds are masters of physical comedy. Their long bodies make every leap, roll, and stretch look exaggerated and hilarious. One moment they're majestically leaping onto the couch; the next, they're stuck halfway because their legs are too short. It's a daily sitcom starring your sausage-shaped friend.

Fact 52: The Art of Dachshund Manipulation

Dachshunds are experts in the art of manipulation. They know exactly how to get what they want, and they're not afraid to use their cuteness as a weapon. With their soulful eyes and adorable head tilts, they can turn even the sternest owner into a puddle of mush.

Let's say you're eating a sandwich, and your dachshund wants a bite. They'll start with a polite stare, then escalate to pawing at your leg. If that doesn't work, they'll let out a pitiful little whine, as if to say, "I haven't eaten in years, please share!" Before you know it, half your sandwich is gone, and your dachshund is looking smug.

The funniest part? They know they've won. Dachshunds have an uncanny ability to look victorious even while chewing. It's like they're silently declaring, "You didn't stand a chance, human."

Fact 53: The Dachshund's Quest for Ultimate Comfort

If there's one thing dachshunds take seriously, it's their comfort. These little dogs will go to great lengths to create the perfect lounging spot. They'll burrow under blankets, rearrange pillows, and even claim your favorite chair as their own.

Once a dachshund has settled into their chosen spot, good luck getting them to move. They'll look up at you with an expression that says, "Do you mind? I was here first." And heaven forbid you try to share the space—they'll stretch out as much as possible to ensure there's no room for anyone else.

It's almost like they have an internal radar for cozy spots. Leave a freshly folded pile of laundry unattended, and your dachshund will be napping on it within seconds. Honestly, they could teach a masterclass in relaxation.

Fact 54: The Dachshund's Obsession with Toys

Dachshunds don't just play with toys—they form emotional attachments to them. Whether it's a squeaky ball, a stuffed animal, or an old sock, dachshunds treat their toys like prized possessions. Some even have a favorite toy that they carry around everywhere, like a toddler with a beloved blankie.

But here's where it gets funny: dachshunds are incredibly possessive of their toys. If another dog (or human) tries to take their toy, they'll unleash their inner drama queen. You might witness a full-blown tantrum, complete with barking, whining, and exaggerated pouting.

And don't even think about throwing their favorite toy away. Dachshunds have an uncanny ability to retrieve "lost" toys, even if they've been hidden in the deepest, darkest corner of the house. It's like they have a sixth sense for squeaky objects.

Fact 55: Dachshunds and Their Love for Sunbathing

If dachshunds had to choose between a gourmet meal and a sunny spot on the floor, the sun would win every time. These little dogs are sun-worshippers through and through. They'll spend hours lying in the sunlight, soaking up the warmth like little solar-powered batteries.

The funny part? They'll move with the sun throughout the day. If a sunbeam shifts an inch, so will your dachshund. By the end of the day, they've practically done a full tour of the house, following the light like a furry little sundial.

But dachshunds don't just lie in the sun—they strike the most dramatic poses while doing it. Picture a sausage dog stretched out like a supermodel, one paw elegantly draped over the other, eyes half-closed in bliss. It's hard not to laugh at their over-the-top love for the simple pleasure of warmth.

Fact 56: Dachshunds and Their Secret Career as Blanket Designers

Dachshunds have an unmatched talent for blanket arrangement. These little pups are essentially interior designers specializing in fabrics, though their focus is less on aesthetics and more on ultimate snuggliness. They will burrow, nudge, tug, and twist blankets until they've created their own masterpiece—a cozy cocoon that only they understand how to enter. The funniest part? No matter how many blankets you provide, they'll always find yours to be superior. You could buy them the plushest, most expensive dog blanket on the market, but your old fleece throw will still be their preferred canvas. Watching a dachshund "construct" their sleeping quarters is like watching a tiny, determined artist at work.

If you try to adjust their handiwork, expect to get a look of utter disdain. In their mind, you've just ruined hours of hard work. Some owners have even noted that their dachshunds seem to "test" different setups before settling in, moving a blanket a millimeter here or there until it's just right.

Fact 57: Dachshunds and Their Fearless Approach to Life

Dachshunds are brave to the point of hilarity. These tiny dogs genuinely believe they are the biggest and toughest creatures on the planet. It doesn't matter if they're facing a vacuum cleaner, a much larger dog, or even a passing shadow—dachshunds will puff out their chest and march into battle like a knight charging into a dragon's lair.

This fearless attitude often leads to some truly laugh-out-loud moments. Imagine a dachshund barking ferociously at a plastic bag blowing in the wind, convinced it's a serious threat. Or watching one try to intimidate a Great Dane, completely unaware of the size difference. Their bravery is both admirable and absurd.

However, their courage does have its limits. The moment they realize the vacuum is actually moving toward them, their bravado disappears, and they scurry away to hide under the couch. But give them a minute, and they're back, ready to "conquer" the world once more.

Fact 58: Dachshunds and Their Inability to Handle Criticism

Dachshunds are incredibly sensitive creatures, especially when it comes to their pride. If you so much as raise an eyebrow at them in disapproval, they'll act as if you've shattered their world. They'll give you the saddest, most heart-wrenching look, complete with drooping ears and big, watery eyes.

But here's where it gets funny: dachshunds also have a flair for the dramatic. If they feel truly wronged, they'll put on a full-blown performance. This might involve flopping onto their side with a dramatic sigh, refusing to make eye contact, or even sulking in a corner. Some owners have even reported their dachshunds turning their back on them as a sign of protest.

The best part? Their "hurt feelings" are almost always short-lived. A belly rub, a treat, or a simple "good dog" is usually all it takes to win them over again. It's as if they have a built-in reset button for their emotions.

Fact 59: Dachshunds and Their Relationship with Food

If there's one thing dachshunds take as seriously as napping, it's eating. These little dogs are absolute food enthusiasts, and they're not picky either. If it's edible (or even if it's not), they'll try to eat it. From sneaking a bite of your sandwich to attempting to swipe an entire pizza slice off the table, dachshunds have an unmatched talent for food theft.

What's truly hilarious is the level of creativity they'll employ to get what they want. Some dachshunds will use their long bodies to their advantage, stretching impossibly far to reach a countertop. Others will employ the "innocent act," pretending they're not interested in your food, only to strike the moment you look away.

Their love for food also makes training them relatively easy. Armed with a pocketful of treats, you can get a dachshund to do almost anything—sit, stay, or even dance on their hind legs. Just don't forget to reward them, or they'll let you know you've failed as a treat-giver with an indignant bark.

Fact 60: Dachshunds and Their Unofficial Role as Alarm Systems

If dachshunds had resumes, "Home Security Specialist" would be at the top of the list. These little dogs take their guard duties very seriously, and they'll alert you to every perceived threat, no matter how insignificant. A mail carrier? Bark. A squirrel in the yard? Bark. A leaf blowing across the driveway? Bark, bark, bark. Their determination to protect their territory is both endearing and exasperating. They'll bark their heads off at a stranger approaching the house, only to immediately turn into a wiggly, tail-wagging mess the moment the person steps inside. It's as if they're saying, "I've done my job; now let's be friends!"

The funniest part is that dachshunds seem to have no concept of size or danger. They'll bark just as fiercely at a butterfly as they would at a burglar. It's this fearless, slightly ridiculous attitude that makes them so lovable—and ensures you'll never miss a single visitor, no matter how small or harmless.

Fact 61: Dachshunds and Their Secret Talent for "Decorating"

Dachshunds have an innate talent for rearranging your home to suit their needs—or so they think. Leave them alone for too long, and you might return to find your couch pillows on the floor, your slippers relocated to their "treasure stash," and a random sock perfectly placed in their bed.

They don't see this as mischief; they're convinced they're helping. Those pillows were clearly in the wrong spot, and your sock? Well, it obviously belongs to them now. Their "decorating" efforts extend to the yard as well. A dachshund will happily dig holes that they believe enhance your garden's aesthetic appeal, often with a wagging tail and dirt-covered snout as they admire their handiwork.

Watching them work is part of the charm. They'll pounce on a pillow, paw at it furiously, then step back to survey their masterpiece. It's a combination of chaos and creativity that only a dachshund can pull off, and you can't help but laugh at their determination.

Fact 62: Dachshunds and Their Love for Fashion

Dachshunds don't just tolerate clothes—they own them. Their unique body shape makes them perfect candidates for stylish outfits, from sweaters to raincoats to Halloween costumes. And while some dogs might sulk when you dress them up, dachshunds often strut around as if they're on a Paris runway.

The funniest part? They seem to have opinions about what they wear. Put them in something they like, and they'll prance around proudly, basking in the compliments. But dare to dress them in an outfit they don't approve of—like an embarrassing reindeer costume for Christmas—and they'll give you a look of pure disdain.

Some dachshunds even develop a preference for certain items, like a favorite sweater they insist on wearing every chilly day. Owners often joke that their sausage dog's wardrobe rivals their own, and honestly, they might not be wrong.

Fact 63: Dachshunds and Their "Selective" Hearing

Dachshunds have a unique relationship with sound. They'll hear the faint crinkle of a treat bag from three rooms away but conveniently "miss" the sound of you calling them when they're busy chasing a squirrel. This selective hearing is both frustrating and hilarious, depending on the situation.

Imagine this: you're trying to get your dachshund to come inside, but they're too focused on sniffing every inch of the backyard. You call their name once, twice, three times—nothing. But the moment you shake their leash or whisper the word "walk," they come bounding toward you like they've been waiting all day to hear those magic words.

Their ability to filter out commands they don't like is almost an art form. It's as if they're thinking, "I'll pretend I didn't hear you, but don't worry, I'm totally listening when it benefits me." And honestly, with those cute floppy ears, it's hard to stay mad at them for long.

Fact 64: Dachshunds and Their Rivalry with Cats

Dachshunds have a love-hate relationship with cats. On one hand, they're fascinated by these mysterious, aloof creatures. On the other hand, they see cats as challengers for attention and territory. The result? A rivalry that's equal parts hilarious and heartwarming.

A dachshund might spend hours trying to outsmart a cat, whether it's by stealing their bed or attempting to play tag (even if the cat isn't interested). The funniest moments happen when the cat outsmarts the dachshund—perching on a high shelf, watching smugly as the dachshund jumps in vain to reach them.

Despite the rivalry, many dachshunds and cats develop a bond over time. You'll catch them snuggling together or teaming up for a shared goal, like convincing you it's dinner time. It's a love-hate dynamic that brings endless entertainment to their humans.

Fact 65: Dachshunds and Their Signature Waddle

One of the most endearing—and funny—things about dachshunds is their unique walk. With their short legs and long bodies, they have a distinctive waddle that's impossible to miss. Watching a dachshund strut down the street is like seeing a tiny, confident parade in motion.

What makes it even better is their attitude. Dachshunds walk like they own the world, chest puffed out and tail wagging proudly. Whether they're heading to the park or just strolling around the living room, they bring a level of swagger that's unmatched by any other breed.

Some owners swear that their dachshunds even "strut" more when they're wearing a new collar or harness. It's as if they know they're looking extra fabulous and want everyone to notice. Their waddle might be a product of their anatomy, but the confidence behind it? Pure dachshund magic.

Fact 66: Dachshunds and Their Obsession with Digging

Dachshunds were originally bred to hunt badgers, and their digging instincts are still alive and well today. Give a dachshund a patch of dirt, and they'll go to town, digging furiously with a look of pure joy on their face.

The funny part? They don't always limit their digging to the outdoors. Some dachshunds will attempt to "dig" into the couch, the carpet, or even your lap. They'll scratch and paw as if they're convinced there's a hidden treasure just beneath the surface.

Owners often joke that their dachshund is training for an excavation career. And while their digging might occasionally cause chaos (like uprooted flowers or a mess of blankets), it's hard not to laugh at their enthusiasm. It's a reminder that even in their cozy modern lives, dachshunds are still adventurers at heart.

Fact 67: Dachshunds and Their "Sausage Stretch"

If you've ever seen a dachshund wake up from a nap, you've likely witnessed the infamous "sausage stretch." It's a full-body performance that involves extending their little legs as far as possible, arching their back, and often letting out a dramatic yawn for good measure. What's so funny about it? For such a small dog, their stretch looks absolutely monumental. It's like they're preparing to tackle the world—or maybe just the next nap. Some dachshunds even add a little wiggle at the end, as if they're resetting their entire sausage-shaped body.

Owners have compared the sight to a cartoon character coming to life. And it's not just cute—it's oddly satisfying to watch. The dachshund stretch has even become a bit of an internet phenomenon, with countless videos showcasing these little dogs perfecting their art of morning (or mid-afternoon) flexibility.

Fact 68: Dachshunds and Their "Short-Legged" Speed Races

Dachshunds might not look like sprinters, but don't let their short legs fool you—they can move fast when they want to. Whether it's chasing a toy, running in circles out of sheer excitement, or making a beeline for the dinner bowl, their bursts of speed are both impressive and hilarious.

What makes it even funnier is the way they run. Their long bodies seem to wiggle in sync with their legs, creating a zigzagging motion that's impossible not to laugh at. And because they're so low to the ground, they almost look like little rockets zooming across the floor.

Dachshund races have even become a popular event at festivals and dog shows. Watching dozens of these tiny sprinters dash toward the finish line, some veering off course or stopping to sniff, is pure comedic gold. It's proof that even the smallest legs can create the biggest laughs.

Fact 69: Dachshunds and Their Love-Hate Relationship with Baths

Bath time with a dachshund is an adventure in itself. While some enjoy the warm water and soothing suds, others act like you've sentenced them to the world's worst punishment. The moment they realize it's bath time, the dramatics begin. Dachshunds will pull out every trick in the book to avoid getting wet—hiding under furniture, giving you the saddest puppy eyes, or suddenly becoming limp noodles when you try to pick them up. Once in the tub, they'll alternate between looking utterly betrayed and splashing water everywhere in an attempt to escape.

The funniest part is their post-bath antics. Once freed, they'll zoom around the house at lightning speed, rubbing against furniture and carpets to "dry off." It's a chaotic and hilarious routine that leaves you laughing, even if you're soaking wet by the end of it.

Fact 70: Dachshunds and Their Surprisingly Loud Voices

For such small dogs, dachshunds have incredibly big voices. Their bark is loud, deep, and surprisingly intimidating—especially when you're not expecting it. In fact, many people are shocked the first time they hear a dachshund bark, wondering how such a tiny body can produce such a powerful sound. Dachshunds use their bark for everything: alerting you to potential "intruders" (like the mail carrier), demanding attention, or simply expressing their excitement. And when they're really passionate about something, they'll let out a series of rapid-fire barks that could rival a much larger dog.

Their vocal talents have earned them the nickname "little hounds with big lungs."

While their barking can sometimes be excessive, it's also part of their charm. After all, a dachshund's bark is just another way of saying, "Hey, I'm here, and I've got something to say!"

Fact 71: Dachshunds and Their "Houdini-Like" Escapes

Never underestimate a dachshund's ability to escape from seemingly secure spaces. These little dogs are surprisingly clever when it comes to finding loopholes—both literal and figurative—in fences, gates, and barriers. Owners have reported dachshunds squeezing through impossibly small gaps, climbing over baby gates, or even digging tunnels worthy of a spy movie. Their determination to explore the great outdoors (or the kitchen) knows no bounds, and they'll stop at nothing to achieve their goal.

What makes their escape attempts so funny is the sheer effort they put into them. A dachshund might spend hours plotting and executing their grand escape, only to get caught and give you an innocent "Who, me?" look. It's equal parts frustrating and hilarious, and it's a reminder of just how smart these little dogs truly are

Fact 72: Dachshunds and Their "Lap Dog" Aspirations

Dachshunds firmly believe they're lap dogs, regardless of whether you're sitting, standing, or lying down. They'll climb onto your lap at the first opportunity, even if it means awkwardly balancing themselves or nudging your laptop out of the way.

Their need to be close to you is both adorable and comedic. Imagine trying to read a book, only to have a dachshund plop themselves right on top of it. Or attempting to work from home, only to find your "assistant" sprawled across your keyboard.

What makes it even funnier is their insistence. If you dare to move them, they'll simply find another way to reclaim their spot. Dachshunds are nothing if not persistent, and their love for lap time is just another way they worm their way into your heart (and your personal space).

Fact 73: Dachshunds and Their "Guard Dog" Personalities

Despite their small size, dachshunds have a natural instinct to protect their family and home. They take their self-assigned role as guard dogs very seriously—sometimes a little too seriously. If a leaf rustles outside, a car passes by, or the neighbor sneezes, your dachshund will sound the alarm.

What's hilarious is the disparity between their size and their confidence. These pint-sized pooches genuinely believe they're fearsome defenders, ready to take on anything. Imagine a 10-pound sausage dog barking ferociously at a delivery driver who's twice their height—it's both brave and absurdly funny.

But beneath their bravado lies a sweet and loyal heart. Dachshunds aren't just barking to be noisy; they genuinely want to keep their loved ones safe. Their over-the-top reactions may leave you laughing, but you'll also feel touched by their devotion.

Fact 74: Dachshunds and Their Love for Blankets

If dachshunds were to create a list of their favorite things, blankets would undoubtedly be at the top. These little burrowers have an innate love for cozying up under layers of fabric, and they'll go to great lengths to find the perfect spot. Don't be surprised if you see your blanket start moving on its own—chances are, there's a dachshund tunneling underneath. They'll twist, turn, and adjust until they're completely cocooned, with just their nose or tail poking out. It's their version of a "sausage roll," and it's absolutely adorable. The funniest part? Once they're snugly tucked in, they'll act as if they own the blanket and glare at you for daring to disturb them. Their love for comfort is unparalleled, and their blanket obsession is just another reason to love these quirky little dogs.

Fact 75: Dachshunds and Their "Selective Hearing"

Dachshunds are smart, but they're also stubborn—especially when it comes to listening. If they don't want to come when called or follow a command, they'll suddenly develop a case of "selective hearing."

What makes it so funny is the way they act. They'll glance at you, acknowledge that they heard you, and then carry on as if nothing happened. It's like they're saying, "I heard you, but I'm choosing to ignore you."

Their stubborn streak can be exasperating, but it's also part of their charm. And let's be honest—who can stay mad at a dachshund when they give you that cheeky, defiant look? It's all part of the sausage dog experience.

Fact 76: Dachshunds and Their Dramatic Side

Dachshunds have a flair for the dramatic. Whether it's a minor inconvenience or a tiny scare, they'll react as if the world is ending. Drop a pillow nearby? They'll jump and give you a look of utter betrayal. Tell them they can't have a bite of your sandwich? They'll let out the most pitiful sigh you've ever heard.

Their melodramatic tendencies make for endless entertainment. Dachshund owners often joke that their dogs deserve an Academy Award for "Best Performance in a Domestic Setting." Every sigh, whine, and exaggerated reaction is worthy of applause.

The best part is that their dramatics often come with a touch of humor. Even when they're sulking, they manage to look so over-the-top that you can't help but laugh. It's all part of their unique personality.

Fact 77: Dachshunds and Their Food Obsession

If there's one thing dachshunds love almost as much as their humans, it's food. These little dogs have an insatiable appetite and an uncanny ability to detect the sound of a snack being opened from miles away.

Their food obsession leads to some hilarious antics. They'll stare at you with laser focus as you eat, sometimes adding dramatic sighs or whines for effect. And if you happen to drop a crumb, they'll pounce on it faster than you can blink. Some dachshunds even develop clever tactics to get more food, like pretending they haven't been fed or mastering the "puppy dog eyes" technique. Their enthusiasm for food is both endearing and laugh-out-loud funny, making every mealtime an adventure.

Fact 78: Dachshunds and Their "Wiggle Walk"

Have you ever noticed how dachshunds walk? Their long bodies and short legs create a signature "wiggle walk" that's both adorable and amusing. As they trot along, their entire body seems to sway in rhythm, creating a charming little dance. The wiggle walk is even more pronounced when they're excited. Whether they're heading to the park, meeting a new friend, or simply going for a car ride, their joyful waddle is enough to make anyone smile. Their unique gait isn't just cute—it's also a reminder of how special dachshunds are. No other dog moves quite like a dachshund, and their wiggle walk is just one more reason why they stand out from the pack.

Fact 79: Dachshunds and Their "Burrowing Olympics"

If burrowing were an Olympic sport, dachshunds would take home the gold every time. This behavior is rooted in their history as hunting dogs—they were bred to dig into burrows in search of prey. Today, that instinct translates into a love for digging, burrowing, and generally getting cozy in tight spaces. Don't be surprised if your dachshund starts rearranging the blankets on your bed or trying to "dig" into your couch cushions. They'll dig with such determination that you'd think they were unearthing buried treasure. And if they can't find a suitable spot to burrow, they might just settle for your laundry pile. The funniest part? Once they're satisfied with their makeshift burrow, they'll pop their head out like a little mole, looking ridiculously proud of their work. Their burrowing obsession is equal parts charming and hilarious, making every day with a dachshund a new adventure.

Fact 80: Dachshunds and Their Unique Sleeping Positions

Dachshunds don't just sleep—they create a spectacle. Whether they're sprawled out on their back, curled into a tiny ball, or contorted into a position that seems physically impossible, their sleeping habits are endlessly entertaining.

One of the most popular dachshund sleeping poses is the "sploot," where they lay flat on their belly with their back legs stretched out behind them. It's both adorable and comical, especially when paired with their signature snoring. Sometimes, they'll even use you as a pillow, draping themselves across your lap or curling up against your side. Their quirky sleeping positions are a constant reminder of their goofy, lovable personalities—and they never fail to make you smile.

Fact 81: Dachshunds and Their Love for Sunbathing

If there's a sunny spot in your house or yard, you can bet a dachshund will find it. These little dogs love nothing more than soaking up the sun, often sprawling out like tiny sausages on a grill.

What makes their sunbathing habit so funny is their complete dedication to it. They'll follow the sun as it moves throughout the day, repositioning themselves to ensure maximum exposure. Some dachshunds even develop a "tan line" on their bellies where their fur is thinner.

Their love for sunbathing is both adorable and relatable. After all, who doesn't enjoy a little relaxation in the sunshine? Just make sure to keep an eye on them, as their enthusiasm for sunbathing can sometimes outweigh their awareness of overheating.

Fact 82: Dachshunds and Their "Prey Drive" Surprises

Dachshunds have a strong prey drive, thanks to their history as hunters. While they may not be chasing down badgers anymore, that instinct still comes out in hilarious and unexpected ways.

For example, your dachshund might suddenly "hunt" a squeaky toy, attacking it with such ferocity that it's hard to believe they're the same dog who was napping five minutes ago. Or they might become laser-focused on a squirrel in the yard, pulling out all the stops to try and catch it—even if it means scaling an improbably tall bush. Their prey drive can lead to some comical moments, like when they mistake a piece of lint for a dangerous intruder or start "stalking" your cat. It's a funny reminder that beneath their sweet, sausage-like exterior lies the heart of a fierce (and slightly silly) hunter.

Fact 83: Dachshunds and Their Signature "Head Tilt"

Few things are as universally adored as a dachshund's head tilt. When they hear something unusual or see something intriguing, they'll cock their head to the side, as if trying to understand what's going on.

The head tilt is both cute and hilarious, especially when paired with their big, soulful eyes. It's almost like they're saying, "Really? Tell me more!" Some dachshunds even take it to the next level, tilting their head back and forth in response to certain sounds or words.

It's a behavior that never fails to melt hearts. And while no one knows exactly why dachshunds do it, one thing's for sure—it's a surefire way to make anyone fall in love with them.

Fact 84: Dachshunds and Their "Zoomies"

When dachshunds get a sudden burst of energy, they enter what's affectionately known as "the zoomies." This involves running around at top speed, often in circles or figure-eights, with no apparent destination in mind.

The zoomies are a sight to behold. Their long bodies and short legs create a wiggling, zigzagging motion that's both chaotic and hilarious. And their sheer enthusiasm is contagious—you can't help but laugh as they race around like tiny, furry tornadoes.

The best part? Dachshunds often look absolutely delighted while zooming, with their tongues hanging out and their tails wagging furiously. It's a pure, unfiltered expression of joy, and it's one of the many reasons why these little dogs are so lovable.

Fact 85: Dachshunds and Their Endless Curiosity

Dachshunds are the Sherlock Holmes of the dog world. They approach life with an insatiable curiosity, always sniffing, investigating, and poking their little noses into everything—sometimes literally. Leave a bag open, and they'll dive right in, emerging with a look that says, "I found treasure!" Open a closet, and they'll trot in like they've discovered a secret portal. Their inquisitive nature is both endearing and hilarious, as it often leads them into situations they weren't entirely prepared for. One of the funniest things about dachshunds is their reaction when they find something unexpected, like a mirror or a vacuum cleaner. They'll tilt their head, bark, or cautiously paw at it, trying to figure out what's going on. Their curiosity keeps life interesting and reminds you to appreciate the little mysteries of the world.

Fact 86: Dachshunds and Their "Doggy Drama"

If dachshunds had a motto, it would probably be "Why be calm when you can be dramatic?" These little dogs have a knack for turning even the smallest inconvenience into a full-blown production.

Tell them they can't go outside, and they'll let out a sigh so deep you'd think they just lost their best friend. Give them a bath, and they'll act like it's the end of the world. Their dramatic flair makes them both challenging and utterly lovable.

One of the funniest examples of dachshund drama is their reaction to being told "no." They'll give you a look of pure betrayal, complete with a huff or a whimper for added effect. It's like living with a tiny, furry soap opera star—and it's impossible not to laugh at their antics.

Fact 87: Dachshunds and Their "Stretch Goals"

Dachshunds are experts in the art of stretching. Thanks to their long, sausage-like bodies, their stretches are both impressive and comical. Whether they're waking up from a nap or preparing for a big adventure, they'll extend their legs and arch their backs in a way that looks almost yogic. The funniest part? They often make dramatic groaning or grunting noises as they stretch, as if they've just finished a marathon (even if they've only walked from the couch to the kitchen). Their exaggerated stretches are a reminder that dachshunds take everything in life—no matter how small—very seriously. Watching a dachshund stretch is oddly therapeutic. Their enthusiasm for such a simple act is infectious, and it's a great reminder to take a moment to stretch and enjoy life's little pleasures.

Fact 88: Dachshunds and Their Unique Vocal Range

Dachshunds may be small, but their barks are anything but. These little dogs have surprisingly deep and loud voices, which often take people by surprise. But barking isn't their only talent—they're also known for their impressive range of whines, grunts, and howls.

What's hilarious is how expressive they are. If they want your attention, they won't just bark—they'll "talk," using a mix of sounds that seem to form a conversation. Some dachshunds even learn to mimic human speech patterns, creating a comical back-and-forth dynamic.

Their vocal abilities are both entertaining and a little baffling. It's as if dachshunds are determined to make their voices heard, no matter the situation. And while their "commentary" can be noisy, it's also a big part of their charm.

Fact 89: Dachshunds and Their "Lap Dog Aspirations"

Dachshunds don't seem to realize their bodies aren't exactly designed for lap-sitting. Despite their long frames and wiggly nature, they're determined to make themselves comfortable on your lap—no matter how awkward the fit.

Their attempts at becoming lap dogs often lead to comical scenarios. They'll twist, turn, and contort themselves until they've found the perfect (and often improbable) position. Sometimes, their entire body won't fit, so they'll settle for draping their front half over your lap while their back half dangles off.

Their love for cuddling is both heartwarming and hilarious. No matter how uncomfortable they look, they'll act like they're in the coziest spot in the world—and they won't hesitate to give you a pouty look if you try to move them.

Fact 90: Dachshunds and Their "Fearless" Approach to Big Dogs

One of the most amusing things about dachshunds is their complete lack of awareness about their size. These tiny dogs have no problem standing up to much larger breeds, often barking or posturing as if they're the toughest dogs in the park.

Their fearless attitude can lead to some laugh-out-loud moments, like when a dachshund challenges a Great Dane or tries to boss around a German Shepherd. The bigger dog is usually so bewildered by the dachshund's audacity that they don't know how to respond.

While their bravery is admirable, it's also a little ridiculous—after all, a dachshund's bark is definitely worse than their bite. But their big personalities are a reminder that confidence comes in all shapes and sizes.

Fact 91: Dachshunds and Their Obsession with Food

If there's one thing dachshunds love more than their humans, it's food. These little sausages are notorious for their insatiable appetites, and they'll stop at nothing to get a taste of whatever you're eating.

Dachshunds have mastered the art of the "puppy dog eyes" routine, staring at you with a mix of hope and desperation that's almost impossible to resist. If that doesn't work, they'll resort to more direct tactics, like pawing at your leg or strategically positioning themselves under the table, ready to catch any crumbs.

The funniest part? Their obsession with food can sometimes lead to some truly ridiculous behavior. They'll raid the trash, attempt daring counter-jumping missions (despite their short stature), or even try to steal food straight from your plate. Their antics are both exasperating and endlessly entertaining—and they're a big reason why dachshunds are such lovable little rascals.

Fact 92: Dachshunds and Their "Blanket Forts"

If dachshunds had a motto, it would be, "Why sleep on a blanket when you can sleep under one?" These little dogs are experts at creating cozy blanket forts, burrowing underneath any available fabric to create their own personal hideaway. Their love for blankets is so strong that they'll often "steal" them from you, tugging and pulling until they've claimed the softest, coziest spot. Once they're nestled in their fort, you might see just a tiny nose or paw poking out, which is both adorable and hilarious.

Watching a dachshund build their blanket fort is like watching a tiny architect at work. They'll scratch, nudge, and rearrange until everything is just right. Their dedication to comfort is truly inspiring—and it's a constant source of amusement for their humans.

Fact 93: Dachshunds and Their Love-Hate Relationship with Water

Dachshunds are an enigma when it comes to water. On one hand, their webbed feet make them surprisingly good swimmers. On the other hand, many dachshunds absolutely hate getting wet.

Bath time, for example, often turns into a dramatic ordeal, complete with whining, squirming, and the occasional escape attempt. Yet, the same dachshund who despises baths might happily splash through puddles or chase after a sprinkler in the yard.

The funniest moments often come at the beach or by the pool. Some dachshunds will cautiously dip a paw into the water, while others will dive in headfirst, only to paddle furiously back to shore. Their unpredictable relationship with water is just another example of their quirky, endearing personalities.

Fact 94: Dachshunds and Their "Nap Time Rituals"

Dachshunds don't just nap—they turn it into a full-blown event. Before settling down for a snooze, they'll often perform an elaborate routine that involves circling their chosen spot, scratching at blankets, and adjusting their position multiple times. Their dedication to finding the perfect napping spot is both amusing and relatable. Sometimes, they'll even try out a few different locations before finally committing, as if they're testing each one for maximum comfort.

Once they've found their ideal spot, they'll curl up in the cutest little ball—or stretch out like a tiny sausage—before letting out a contented sigh. Watching a dachshund prepare for a nap is oddly entertaining, and it's a reminder that sometimes, it's worth taking a little extra time to get comfortable.

Fact 95: Dachshunds and Their "Sausage Dog Races"

Did you know there are actual races dedicated to dachshunds? Known as "wiener dog races," these events are both hilarious and heartwarming, as dozens of dachshunds compete to see who can reach the finish line first.

What makes these races so funny is that dachshunds aren't exactly built for speed. Their short legs and long bodies create a wiggly, almost comical running style—and some of them get so distracted along the way that they forget they're supposed to be racing.

Despite the chaos, wiener dog races are a celebration of everything that makes dachshunds special: their quirky personalities, their determination, and their ability to bring people together. Whether they win or lose, every dachshund who participates is a champion in their own right.

Fact 96: Dachshunds and Their "Tail Wagging Adventures"

A dachshund's tail is more than just a tail—it's a barometer of their mood, a tool for communication, and occasionally, a source of unintentional comedy.

When a dachshund is excited, their tail wags with such intensity that their entire body starts to wiggle. It's like watching a furry little metronome, and it's impossible not to smile at their enthusiasm. On the flip side, their tail can also be hilariously stubborn—like when it gets stuck under a couch cushion, and they spend several minutes trying to free it.

The funniest moments often happen when dachshunds get a case of "tail chases." They'll spin in circles, trying to catch their own tail, completely oblivious to the fact that it's attached to their body. Their tail-wagging adventures are a constant source of joy and laughter.

Fact 97: Dachshunds and Their "Protective Instincts"

Despite their small size, dachshunds take their role as protectors very seriously. They'll bark at anything and everything they perceive as a threat, from delivery drivers to squirrels to harmless inanimate objects.

What's hilarious is how over-the-top their protective instincts can be. They'll puff out their chest, lower their body, and bark with such determination that you'd think they were guarding a royal palace. And if the "threat" doesn't back down, they'll escalate to more dramatic tactics, like hopping or doing an exaggerated "attack" pose.

While their protective instincts can be a bit excessive at times, they're also incredibly endearing. After all, dachshunds just want to keep their humans safe—even if it means barking at a suspicious-looking leaf.

Fact 98: Dachshunds and Their "Famous Fans"

Over the years, dachshunds have gained a loyal following among celebrities, artists, and even royalty. Notable dachshund enthusiasts include Andy Warhol, who had two dachshunds named Archie and Amos, and Pablo Picasso, whose dachshund Lump appeared in several of his paintings.

Queen Victoria was also a fan of the breed, helping to popularize them in England during the 19th century. And today, celebrities like Adele, Jack Black, and Josh Duhamel are proud dachshund owners. The funniest part about dachshunds' celebrity connections is how their quirky personalities often seem to overshadow their famous owners. After all, who wouldn't be captivated by a sassy little sausage dog?

Fact 99: Dachshunds and Their "Fashion Sense"

Dachshunds have become unexpected icons in the world of pet fashion, thanks to their unique body shape and undeniable charisma. From cozy sweaters to elaborate costumes, dachshunds can pull off just about any look—and they know it.

What's hilarious is how dachshunds seem to embrace their role as fashionistas. Many of them will strut around in their outfits with a level of confidence that would put runway models to shame. Some even develop preferences for certain clothing items, like a favorite hoodie or a particularly dashing bowtie.

The annual Halloween costume contests are a spectacle to behold. Dachshunds have been dressed as hot dogs (of course), superheroes, tacos, and even famous historical figures. Their willingness to humor their owners' sartorial whims is just another reason why these little dogs are so endlessly entertaining.

Fact 100: Dachshunds and Their "Infinite Charm"

If there's one thing every dachshund owner can agree on, it's that these little dogs have a seemingly endless supply of charm. Whether they're making you laugh with their antics, warming your heart with their affection, or surprising you with their intelligence, dachshunds have a way of leaving a lasting impression.

Part of their charm lies in their contradictions: they're tiny yet fearless, stubborn yet lovable, and mischievous yet incredibly loyal. They're the kind of dogs who'll steal your socks one minute and snuggle up with you the next, completely winning you over in the process. The funniest part? Dachshunds are fully aware of their charm and aren't afraid to use it to their advantage. Whether they're begging for treats, vying for attention, or trying to get out of trouble, they'll flash you a look that's impossible to resist. It's their world—we're just living in it.

Fact 101: Dachshunds and Their Legacy – A Tail Wagging Through History

Dachshunds aren't just dogs; they are legends with wagging tails and paws that have left indelible marks on the sands of time. From their humble beginnings as hunters in the forests of Germany to becoming cherished members of royal families and Hollywood stars, these little dogs have done it all. Did you know that the dachshund has inspired not only art and music but even political movements? During World War I, the dachshund became a symbol of resilience, enduring through adversity with their heads held high (and ears flopping adorably). In modern times, dachshunds have earned a reputation as mascots of determination. Whether it's their relentless pursuit of a tennis ball under the couch or their unwavering loyalty to their humans, they remind us that size truly doesn't matter when it comes to heart and spirit. They've been the muses for authors, the stars of viral internet memes, and even the faces of quirky merchandise ranging from coffee mugs to socks.

And let's not forget their special gift of bringing people together. Dog parks, dachshund races, and even global social media groups are buzzing with people celebrating their shared love for this iconic breed. With their endless antics, affectionate cuddles, and occasionally stubborn streaks, dachshunds have taught us to cherish the simple joys in life—like a sunbeam on the carpet or a good belly rub.

Fact 101 isn't just about the dachshund; it's about their legacy. They've earned their spot as a timeless symbol of love, loyalty, and laughter—one wag at a time.

Printed in Great Britain
by Amazon